Forgiveness

inSIGHTS

BIBLE STUDIES FOR GROWING
FAITH

Susan K. Williams Smith

THE PILGRIM PRESS
Cleveland

Dedication

This book is dedicated to Diane Williams,
who has shown forgiveness by her very walk with God.

The Pilgrim Press, 700 Prospect Avenue, Cleveland, Ohio 44115-1100
pilgrimpress.com
© 2003 by The Pilgrim Press

Biblical quotations are from the New Revised Standard Version of the Bible, © copyright 1989 by the Divisions of Christian Education of the National Council of the Churches of Christ in the U.S.A., and are used by permission.

Printed in the United States of America on acid-free paper

08 07 06 05 04 03   5 4 3 2 1

Smith, Susan K. Williams, 1954 –
    Forgiveness / Susan K. Williams Smith.
    p. cm. – (Insights: Bible studies for growing faith)
    ISBN 0-8298-1579-1 (pbk. : alk. paper)
    1. Bible O.T. Forgiveness – Biblical teaching. 2. Forgiveness – Religious aspects – Christianity. I. Forgiveness II. Insights (Cleveland, Ohio)

BS680.F64S65 2003
234'.5–dc22   2003055541

Contents

Introduction

I suppose every Christian has his or her pet peeve. You know, that "something" that is or is not happening within the faith that just gets one's gall. The plethora of Christian denominations attests to the same. It is quite amazing and amusing to think that the thousands of denominations claim to have the "one up" on what is ultimately right and true.

One supposes that the debates over what is "the truth" began even as Jesus walked the earth, and certainly, the debates increased after his untimely death. The most ironic reality about the debates, however, is that it seems that Jesus' ultimate messages never really took hold of our spirits – not even that of his Disciples. Jesus fought hard with his words and his actions to get people to de-emphasize legalism. He also worked hard to get people to embrace a gospel which really casts a pall on the pre-eminent importance of legalism in the eyes of God. Jesus wanted us to work on our characters and he clearly indicated that one's character is on the inside. It's the character that God sees, Jesus intimated, not one's position or how well one obeyed moralistic laws. In fact, Jesus suggested that merely following all of the laws was not enough to get close to God.

So, Jesus gave us hard words, simple, but hard words by which to live. They are found throughout the Gospels. One might call them "lessons for character building," or "ways to get into the realm of God," and they are as powerful and effective as any Tony Robbins seminar. Yet, we as Christians too often ignore them. They are distasteful. More than that, they go against the human grain. If the truth be told, we are more comfortable being human than we are seeking God's realm — especially if seeking involves doing all the things Jesus asks us to do!

People, including Christians, carry around and sometimes incubate and protect, the so called "things of the flesh." Some of those fleshly possessions or attributes are listed in Galatians 5: "fornication, impurity, licentiousness, idolatry, sorcery, enmities, strife, jealousy, anger, quarrels, dissensions, factions, envy, drunkenness, carousing, and things like these." (Galatians 5:20–21) Because of the gift of grace, we very often excuse ourselves for our indiscretions, relying on the belief that once we have decided to follow Jesus, we are saved. We excuse our weaknesses and proclaim that after all, Jesus has convinced us that God forgives us. So the truth of the matter is that too often, we simply allow our flesh to have dominance in our lives.

But Jesus' gospel clearly admonishes us to seek a higher existence and to follow what he says in order to be able to realize that existence. It is what he says that gets us, because it's too hard! — loving one's enemies; turning the other cheek when offended; and not seeking revenge when wronged. Equally important, Jesus has asked us to forgive those who have hurt us — and hurt us bad.

This Bible study is a discussion on forgiveness. It is not a popular thing for Christians to discuss. Yet, if we are serious about the Christian walk, we have to incorporate Jesus' command into our daily life. It is not easy to do, nor is it palatable. Sometimes, it is infuriating to know that Jesus demands forgiveness in light of the wrongs done to us. Jesus knew our reaction would not be favorable toward this command, however, he didn't remove it from his requirements for us. All of us have reasons why forgiveness is not an option at this point. Some of us, maybe too many of us, have reasons why forgiveness is not an option for something done a long time ago. And too many of us are not even close to considering the forgiveness option.

Regardless of our resistance, the command stands. Now, as Christians, we can choose whether or not we want to obey Jesus' commands. God gave us the wonderful gift of free will, and we exercise our options. But it would appear that there is a serious price for exercising the "I'm not going to do it" option, and that price is spelled out in the Bible itself.

"Not everyone who says to me, 'Lord, Lord,' will enter the kingdom of heaven, but only the one who does the will of my father in heaven." (Matthew 7:21) That's what Jesus said. I believe that's what Jesus meant.

Jesus' Intent

When one reads through the commands of Jesus, it is tempting to ask, "What was his intent?" Didn't he know he was asking something that was nearly impossible for humans to do? Why then would he ask us to forgive people? People who have broken our hearts, our trust, our confidence?

He asked it so that we might experience peace on earth. It's not just a phrase. It's a way of life. And what Jesus wanted was for us to understand that fact and to experience the joy of salvation while we were yet alive.

We would argue the logic of his desire. Jesus may have had the ability to forgive the people who hurt him but he is the Son of God. We think that God must have given him something special in order to do what we cannot do. Surely that is the case.

But we forget that Jesus was both divine and human, and that reality presupposes that Jesus experienced the same struggles that we as humans experience when we really try to do God's will.

Jesus came to shake up the status quo and to create a new reality. This new reality, however, was not for his sake, nor was it for his benefit. It was for ours. Jesus knew that some of us carry around the torment for years, while others, carry it their entire lives. And because he was compassionate and knew that torment is a natural barrier to experiencing God's peace and presence, Jesus gave us a soul prescription that was guaranteed to produce spiritual healing.

Like any medicine that will bring healing, Jesus' elixir does not "taste" good and is therefore subject to rejection far too often. When we are physically ill, many of us would rather let nature take its course than take a foul-tasting medicine, no matter how good it is purported to be. Some of us take pills to be healed – avoiding the bitter taste of the liquid.

Jesus' command to forgive, however, is not in pill form. It is a spiritual liquid that absolutely violates our sense of what we can endure. Though we are infected with the disease of non-forgiveness, many of us would rather suffer and hurt than take the bitter directive which promises to bring healing.

It is a normal human reaction. We want things to be easy, and forgiveness is not easy to do. When the Israelites were being led to the Promised Land through the wilderness, they balked when the journey became difficult and actually voiced their desire to return to captivity rather than follow the torturous and unknown course to deliverance. "But the people were thirsty for water there and they grumbled against Moses. They said, 'Why did you bring us out of Egypt, to kill us and our children and livestock with thirst?'" (Exodus 17:3) The journey had gotten difficult and the people were tired. They had forgotten how miserable they had been in Egypt and actually longed to go back to their captivity and pain rather than follow God's messenger!

We are still the same. We balk at Jesus' incredible commands and some of us actually make the decision to remain in pain rather than trust Jesus through the wilderness on the way to spiritual freedom. We "murmur" against Jesus and therefore against God, even as we continue to complain about our pain. What else is it but a complaint when we say we can't get to God or that God hasn't heard us?

Jesus' intent is that we are freed of the burden of carrying anger and pain we've carried so long. That's why He said, "Take my yoke upon you, and learn from me; for I am gentle and humble in heart, and you will find rest for your souls." (Matthew 11:29) It's simply too much to carry, and it is an impediment to being in right relationship with God.

Understand this: nothing about what Jesus commands of us makes human sense. It is a spiritual walk. This is why Scripture says that God is a spirit, and those who worship him must worship in spirit and truth. (John 4:24) There is nothing logical or rational about what Jesus commands. In order to receive Jesus fully, we must be willing to let go of our very human nature.

The cost of not letting go of our human will and deciding to hold on to issues that make us cringe is death of the soul. Our refusal "to let go and let God be God" is like refusing manna from heaven. Our spirits are starved for peace and comfort. It is a peace and comfort which only God can give. Jesus hopes we'll realize that before it's too late — before we find ourselves at death's door — still bitter, angry, and spiritually compromised. His intent is that we will let go of our humanness and let God be God.

Questions for Reflection and Discussion:

1. Identify the thing or things that have happened in your life for which you've been unable to offer forgiveness.

2. What have you gained by not forgiving? What have you lost?

3. Have you ever considered the possibility that holding onto your anger is a sin? If you were to realize that it is a sin, would your desire to forgive increase? Why or why not?

4. What have you always thought of Jesus' command to forgive? Have you ever thought it pertained to you?

5. Read the story of the Israelites' journey through the wilderness in Exodus. Can you see any parallels between their protest of God's direction and your own?

6. Do you believe that it is Jesus' intent that you be free of pain? Why or why not?

7. Do you think your unwillingness to forgive jeopardizes your salvation in any way? Why or why not?

A Sin is a Sin

"Not everyone who says, 'Lord, Lord,' will enter the kingdom of heaven." Jesus said it. And what will keep some of us out will be our unwillingness and failure to follow God's will. It follows, then, that those of us who are not willing to forgive are in a bit of a bind.

We have to presume that what Jesus commanded us to do is the will of God. Jesus continually said that what he said was the will of "the one who sent me." God sent God's son as an example of what we are to do. If we want to gain entrance into the realm of God, we should do God's will.

We get caught up in defining and rating sins. In our humanness, though we will readily say, "love the sinner and hate the sin," that's not entirely true. We love SOME sinners. Some of them we have relegated to the "lost" category. We blatantly call out those whom we deem to have offended God the most – such as homosexuals; those who have abortions; and those who don't raise their kids the way we think they should.

We omit other sins such as child abuse, adultery, lying, cheating, acting on jealous impulses, displaying envy, getting drunk (we lift drinking up as a national past time!), cheating, and gambling. Through our very narrow window of definition, we humans have decided and decreed what a sin is.

We forget the basic definition of sin. Sin is anything that separates us from God. And those things include anger, rage, envy, jealousy, judging others, gambling, cheating, coveting someone else's spouse or material possessions, eating too much, violating our bodies, the temple of God, and worshipping money. The list goes on and on. Anything into which we put more energy than our relationship to God is a sin.

Not being able to forgive is a spiritual disease. Not being willing to forgive is a sin. Whenever your basic peace is disturbed by your human inclinations, you are, we are, out of the will of God and therefore in sin. That's what sin does. A sin is much more than being "good" or "bad." A sin is a spiritual parasite that robs us of spiritual nutrients, sucking our life blood until one day we realize we are dead inside. How else might we explain so-called "good" people who are completely miserable? There are a lot of people who appear to follow all of the laws and rules of the church who cannot find peace. They are what I call, spiritually anemic.

Jesus understood the dilemma in which Christians find themselves. In Matthew 12:1–13, there is a story involving Jesus and the Pharisees. The Pharisees were good rule-followers. They knew all the laws. They thought it sacrilege for people to break the rules, no matter the situation.

Jesus and his disciples were in the grain fields picking heads of grain as the disciples were hungry. The Pharisees were aghast! It was the Sabbath, and picking the heads of grain was considered work; no one was to work on the Sabbath. Not only were the Pharisees upset that the disciples were picking the grain, they were even more upset that Jesus was allowing it! They were immediately accusatory. They said, "Look, your disciples are doing what is not lawful to do on the Sabbath." (Matthew 12:2)

Jesus goes through a lengthy discussion, letting the Pharisees know that he knew the law and the history of his people. Jesus was also aware of what David did and said when he had entered God's house on a day it was deemed unlawful to do so. He let the Pharisees know that he knew they didn't have a clue about what God requires — mercy, not sacrifice — things of the spirit, not things of the flesh.

The Pharisees are, of course, not appeased. They ask him, "Is it lawful to cure on the Sabbath? For by this time, they had moved on and were faced with a man who had a shriveled hand. Jesus asks them a very basic question: "Suppose one of you had only one sheep and it falls into a pit on the Sabbath; will you not lay hold of it and lift it out? How much more valuable is a human being than a sheep! So it is lawful to do good on the Sabbath." (Matthew 12:11–12)

Against the gasps of the Pharisees, Jesus healed the man's hand. The Pharisees declared Jesus the sinner. But it was they who were in sin because their human feelings, beliefs, and inclinations kept them separated from God. Their humanness kept them from experiencing and sharing in God's mercy.

A sin is a sin. Humans, for all of our efforts, don't have the qualifications to declare what a sin is, nor do we have the ability to be able to tell who's going to heaven and who's not. One thing is clear, though: Sin is a barrier between us and God, and it's the barriers that keep us out of God's realm.

Jesus' intent is for us to be able to enter God's realm. Sin will keep us out. Being unwilling to forgive is a sin. We would balk at such a pronouncement; we would cry, "But he/she hit me first!" Unfortunately, Jesus' teachings don't allow us the luxury of wallowing in anger, bitterness or resentment just because we were wronged first.

If we go back to his teachings, we see it: "Whenever you stand praying, forgive, if you hold anything against anyone; so that your Father in heaven may also forgive you your trespasses." (Mark 11:25) In Matthew, the command is expanded, so as not to leave us with any questions: "So when you are offering your gift at the altar, if you remember that your brother or sister has something against you, leave your gift there before the altar and go; first be reconciled to your brother or sister and then come and offer your gift." (Matthew 5:23–24)

So, Jesus is saying, it really doesn't matter if "he" or "she" hit you, hurt you, betrayed you, first. The command is to settle the matter. Be reconciled. Let go of your need to "get him/her" back. Otherwise you are in sin.

It never ceases to amaze me that Christians somehow don't get it. We spend so much time worrying about outward behavior and appearances of others that we really leave a lot of sin unnoticed and unspoken. Our human minds totally reject the notion that we could be in sin when someone else has hurt us. And yet, the command to forgive remains.

We, God's people, have always asked for forgiveness and have always been glad God has done just that. All through the Old Testament, the people of God asked for forgiveness, in spite of doing absolutely heinous things. The people asked, and the God of the Old Testament complied. David asked in Psalm 51:"Have mercy on me, O God, according to your steadfast love; according to your abundant mercy blot out my transgressions." (Psalm 51:1)

It's what David says near the end of this Psalm that I think God wants us to understand. Psalm 51:17 reads: "The sacrifice acceptable to God is a broken spirit; a broken and contrite heart, O God, you will not despise."

David realized that he had to have a broken spirit in order to humble himself enough to ask God for forgiveness. He realized that sacrifices and other similar acts would not work. It doesn't matter how many external things we might do that have the appearance of forgiveness. God is interested in the movement of one's heart —

from a place of hardness and bitterness to a place of spiritual pliability — one where God can enter and become outwardly manifested by a merciful spirit.

Not allowing God into one's heart is a sin. The ability to forgive is impossible without having God's love in one's heart. God in one's heart breaks the molds; breaks through all of the old garbage that has petrified over time; and has spoiled our spirits.

One cannot be a Christian and not let God into one's heart.

We therefore must forgive the "biggies" in our lives. If we are Christian, we must forgive the husbands, lovers, friends, wives, best friends, colleagues, children, parents...all those who have broken our hearts in a million pieces.

Sin, is the unwillingness to forgive.

Questions for Reflection and Discussion

1. Discuss Mark 11:25. What is Jesus saying to you in this passage of scripture?

2. Discuss Matthew 5:23–24. How does this passage of scripture relate to the passage in Mark?

3. Who "hit you first" in your life? If you feel comfortable, name the person and discuss the situation that has left you unable to forgive.

4. What do you think about non-forgiveness as a sin? If it isn't a sin, what is it?

5. Discuss Psalm 51. Review the circumstances of David's life that led him to write this Psalm.

6. Do you think God will forgive you of your sins if you do not forgive the people who have hurt you?

7. Devise a "Biblical Action Plan" that you could follow to help you get to the point where you can forgive those who have hurt you.

8. What do you think might be the consequences for one who is unwilling to forgive?

The Process of Forgiveness

It's not going to happen overnight.

Sometimes, the process of forgiveness can take forever, depending on what the hurt was, and who did it.

There's an emotional sequence of events that happens when a human being has been hurt. We can call them "stages of pain."

The first stage of pain is shock and denial. Surely this person did not do this or say this to me. It's hard for us to conceptualize that anyone could or would do some of the things we do to each other, especially in the name of love, or under the rubric of love. We think love won't let parents desert their children; love won't let a spouse be unfaithful; love won't let a best friend betray a friend; love won't let a child disrespect the parents who raised him/her; love won't let a person tell an outright lie on another one. This is how we think.

Human behavior often ekes out the winning run when emotions and needs and wants are involved. Human behavior drives us to do unthinkable acts. So when human behavior wins out, as it so often does, our spiritual cores shrink back in pain and disbelief. We go into denial about how bad we really feel; perhaps it's that we hurt so bad we cannot even get to the pain. Whatever the reason or scenario, the first step in the stages of pain is shock and denial.

The second stage of pain is what I call the "oozing" phase. In this stage of pain, bits and pieces of what has just happened tear away from the whole and begin to ooze into our spirits. It doesn't happen all at once. It just oozes. And each drop takes us deeper and deeper into an emotional abyss. We begin to really think about what was said or done, or about who said it. In this oozing phase, we can see their faces, hear their voices, and remember word for word what we heard. We wish the oozing would stop, because the more "it" oozes, the more we hurt or the angrier we become. But it doesn't stop. It continues to cast a pall over our spirits, until the thoughts of what happened to us or what was done to us consume us.

The third stage of pain is the "attack" phase. It is in this stage that our human resolve to "get even" or "get back" at someone begins to evolve. It is a strong emotion and quite powerful. During this phase, we want to say something or do something to let the other person or persons know that they have hurt us.

Interestingly, the behaviors we exhibit during the attack phase are not particularly gratifying. In fact, what likely happens is that the offender says or does something that increases the ire of the one who was initially hurt. Thus, the feeling of being wounded and wronged becomes deeper, and a rage grows within that spreads like a cancer. It eats our joy, our capacity to feel, our attention. It is the manifestation of the illness of not forgiving.

But it is at this stage that illness turns into sin. The wounded feelings become so consummate that we lose our desire to let go of it all. We are so much more concerned with protecting our human need for respect and honor, and the need to show our power by getting the person back who got us, that we lose sight of God. We cannot see God and we choose not to hear God. Our attitude is most often that God understands our feeling and is probably sympathetic with it. We abandon the words of the gospels that command us to forgive and we press forward to satisfy a human pain which only God and God's solutions can assuage.

Since our pain gets to where it is via process, it makes sense that it takes a similar process to remove it. The only antidote to emotional and spiritual pain is forgiveness. This kind of pain is like a spiritual infection. In cases of physical infection, only an antibiotic will get rid of the harmful bacteria. For spiritual infections, forgiveness acts like an antibiotic, effectively killing the human bacteria which keep us captive to our human urge not to forgive. It seems that as long as we refuse to listen to God or obey God's commands, the spiritual illness is like a virus; it repels the Word of God and its promise of healing. As soon as we let go of our desire to get the other person back, however, it is as though the virus converts to a bacterial infection which does in fact respond to the treatment pre-scribed by God. In the viral state, no spirit can be healed. The feelings of pain and anger and bitterness do not go away, but instead intensify over time. Only when we relent, when we trust that God's words are more powerful than our solutions, can the healing begin.

Some of us do not want to be healed. We, therefore, will not enter into the process. Some of us will agree to relent for certain instances of abuse and bad treatment, but not for others. So, we live half healed and half sick. It is like having a cold that never goes away. Those who trust in God, however, can feel the release God gives.

The first stage of forgiveness is acknowledging that there is indeed a reason we need God. Many of us do not call on God when we feel hurt. We won't admit there's a problem. There is a problem, and until we admit it, we cannot begin to be treated.

The second stage of forgiveness is a conscious state-ment to God that we need God's intervention. We can not do it by ourselves. We will fail every time we think about how bad we hurt and what the other person did. The con-scious statement to God makes us say out loud what our spirits beg us to say. Understand that this statement to God is a spiritual and not a physical phenomenon. It represents a level of trust that is just enough to get us past our human inclinations.

The third stage of forgiveness is recognition that we will not be able to forgive if we spend all of our time practicing how the other person has hurt us. We have to acknowledge that there is possibly something even in our reaction to an event which is preventing us from getting to and hearing from God. Blaming the other person only makes us feel self-righteous and keeps us far away from the desire to forgive. If we can humble ourselves before God and admit that we, like those who have hurt us, need forgiveness, God will begin to break the shell of resistance.

Once we begin these three stages, the process is underway. Bit by bit, we will find that God will release us from our angst, our tension, and our painful recollections. God allows the wounded to first begin to function, and then live, fully knowing that the situation is in God's hands. It is the work of God — the spiritual antibiotics — that attacks the germs that infect us and keep us from joy.

In the Bible, we can see the result of the one who has entered into the process of forgiveness and the one who apparently is not willing to do so in the same story. It is the all-too-familiar story of the Prodigal Son. At the end of the story, when the wayward son decides to come home, the wounded father receives him with joy and love. Never mind that the son disrespected and abandoned the father's home; never mind that the son squandered money; and never mind that the son had been self-centered and self-serving, not caring who he hurt as he satisfied his desires. Surely, the father had been advised not to allow his son to return. Surely, he had been admonished for being a fool in giving this son anything at all, as the son had never shown a sizeable degree of responsibility. Surely, this father had been chastised by friends and family alike.

But at the end of the story, the wayward son is on his way home and the wounded father is waiting for him, waiting to give him the best of everything. He is joyous. The antibiotics that only God can apply had worked for this man, who could have turned into a very bitter and vindictive person. The antibiotics had allowed the father to enter into the process of forgiveness, so that when the son returned, the father could receive him.

On the other hand, this was not the case with the elder son. The elder son felt angry and betrayed by his brother's sudden reappearance. To this son, it appeared that the younger son was up to his old tricks. How many times had the elder brother had to cover for the antics of his younger brother? How many times had the elder son gone without because of the crying and whining of the younger son? How many times had the younger son even snubbed the elder son for being so "self righteous" and being unable to get away with what he did? How many times had the elder son watched in anger as the younger son got his way, over and over again?

When the younger son left, we can imagine that the elder son was happy. He was glad that the "trouble" of the house was out of the way. Surely now his father would give him his due, his rewards, for being "good." Surely when or if the younger son reappeared he would be put in his place and the elder son, who had been responsible throughout, would be praised and finally recognized?

When it didn't happen, the older son sunk into an abyss of anger. He had no intention of forgiving his brother, even if his father was stupid enough to do so. He seethed as he watched his father dance about, preparing for his brother's return. Not only was this brother getting good treatment, he was getting the "best" of everything! Where was the justice in it all? Why couldn't his father see what a fool of himself he was making? His father wanted him to rejoice, but the older son had no intentions of doing it. He wanted his brother to get what was owed him — and that certainly wasn't the fatted calf! The father had already been engaged in the process of forgiveness. The older son, however, had been spiritually ill and now in sin: not being able to forgive at first and now, not wanting do. One person's process was toward healing; the other's process was toward spiritual ruination.

It is incumbent upon all of us to decide which process we want to enter into. One leads to closeness to God and release from the shackles of spiritual illness. The other leads us away from God and keeps a barrier between us and God which only makes us more spiritually ill on a daily basis. The choice is ours.

Questions for Reflection and Discussion

1. At this very moment, what is keeping you from entering the process of forgiveness?

2. What do you think you would lose if you forgave the person for whom you hold bad feelings today?

3. Study the story of the Prodigal Son in Luke 15:11. To what would you attribute the behavior of the elder son?

4. Have you been trying to forgive someone for some time now with no luck? Write down the reasons why you think you're stuck. What would you like to see happen to the person who has hurt you?

5. Look at Psalm 35:1. Could you pray this Bible verse and feel confident that God would take care of your enemies? Would that assurance be enough for you?

6. In your opinion, are there times when God would not require you to forgive someone? List those times.

7. If you had to identify the stage of pain in which you are in now, where would it be?

8. What are the physical manifestations of not forgiving someone? Have you experienced any of these?

9. "To not forgive someone, or to not be willing to forgive someone, is an indication of one's distrust of God." Do you agree or not agree with this statement? Give your reasons.

10. Write down an instance where you did forgive someone. What were the results for you personally? Are you happy or sorry you forgave him or her? How long did it take you?

Count It All Joy

There is nobody who understands how God works. We try to shape God our way; we put onto God and into God the ways of human beings. We might not do it purposely, but we do, just the same.

So when "bad" things happen to us, we react with human wailing and expect God to honor that wailing. When something happens to us that breaks our hearts, we lash out at God for letting it happen and think that it is a "bad" thing in our lives. This way of thinking comes out of our belief that if we are God's, then we deserve special treatment. We think there ought to be perks for believing in God; for confessing Jesus; for going to church; and serving. It goes beyond the pale of human comprehension that our God would allow suffering in our lives when we've tried to be "good" servants or followers.

Why else would the Psalmist write, "Do not fret because of the wicked; do not be envious of wrongdoers." (Psalm 37:1) The Psalmist is addressing our confusion about how could a just and good God allow God's followers to suffer as they do ... while simultaneously apparently letting the "bad guys" get away with murder. Even though a "bad" thing might have been allowed for our good, it does not assuage our resentment at the thing being allowed to happen at all. Let's face it, when bad things happen to us, it challenges our beliefs about God. God couldn't be good and all powerful because God would not have allowed the bad thing to happen to us. Or, by sheer might, God could have prevented it. We think that way. Thinking either way brings us to a crisis of faith which poses a problem when we are wrestling with the issue of forgiveness.

But there is a truth about "bad" experiences that we cannot let slip by. Sometimes, the worst things that happen to us, the biggest betrayals, the most painful experiences, are for our own good. Could it be that God allows us to experience some of the bad things so that ultimately we are better servants for God?

Recently, I was deeply hurt by a colleague whom I felt snubbed me. It was so painful that I could hardly talk about it. I resolved that I would never support this colleague again. I thought that she had been rude and insensitive.

Later, I had an opportunity to talk with her and asked her some advice about pastoral issues. She is a very successful pastor. Even though I was angry and hurt, I listened to her, and resolved to put her suggestions to use.

As I have followed her advice, I have come to understand that the rebuff in and of itself was not a bad thing. It happened for a reason and for me to continue to hold it against her would work against me. I have heard that "still, small voice" whispering to me to forgive her and move on, and I recently wrote her a letter thanking her for her advice. Whew! That was God for sure! To write someone whom you know has no use for you but who helped is an awesome experience. When I was initially hurt, I resolved that I would not talk to her again. We did, however, and I have benefited greatly. The act of forgiveness was not for her sake; it was for mine.

Yet another case involves a member who has since moved away but who again, hurt me immensely. Before she left, however, she gave me some advice which again, was powerful and positive. I have to admit, concerning this member, I am in the midst of the forgiveness process. I have not yet written her nor do I want to tell her how much she hurt me and more importantly, how much she helped me. But I realize, again, that I must "count it all joy" that she and I had the relationship we did, and that she felt she could and should share with me what she did. My not being able or willing to forgive her is stealing my joy, not hers.

It is written in the book of James: "My brothers and sisters, whenever you face trials of any kind, consider it nothing but joy." (James 1:2–3) In other words, the bad things in our lives can either kill us or energize us spiritually. If we look on the bad thing or the painful thing as just bad, we will wither away spiritually. So much of our energy will be spent on thinking about the person who hurt us, wondering why he or she did what he or she did, and wanting to "get even." This is the "interference" that gets between us and God and which thus qualifies non-forgiveness as a sin.

If we, however, look on the bad thing as a lesson, our attitudes change. I once heard Deepak Chopra say that bad things are lessons, are instructional, and are therefore not bad. When we are able to look on the "bad" thing as a lesson, our spiritual energy absorbs the lesson and we spend far less time feeling bad.

It's a miracle, for sure.

If we look further in the passage from James, we see that he says, "…and let endurance have its full effect, so that you may be mature and complete, lacking in nothing. (James 1:4). The scripture gives a reason why Jesus commanded us to forgive: He wants us to be mature and complete, not lacking anything – not joy, not peace, not understanding, not closeness to him, nothing. If we're able to look on our pain in that way, it changes the way we handle it.

No person alive understands the way God works, and why God works as God does. But the truth remains that God's commands are not superfluous. They work for our spiritual betterment.

When we can "count it all joy," the pain against us pales in comparison to the joy we receive as we let go of our desire to hurt. Not forgiving means on one level that we have chosen to hurt, as opposed to heal. When, however, we can develop and trust an understanding or a hunch that "God is in this someplace," it takes the pressure off us. We realize we don't have to hold a grudge to feel vindicated. We understand that God will take care of our spirits and the other person or persons as well. It'll happen in God's time, but we know that it will happen, and we are at rest, in spite of the pain.

One other thing, we should say: This feeling of joy is spiritual, not temporal at all. It is different from being "happy." The Greek root of the word "happy" is "hap," which means "chance." Being happy is subject to the winds of change. One can be happy one moment and miserable the next because happiness is fleeting by virtue of its dependence on outside circumstances.

Joy is a deeper emotion, a spiritual "place," if you will, that is given by God and therefore is untouchable by human wiles and situations. One can have joy while he or she watches a loved one die. One is sad because that loved one is about to depart earth, but feels joy from having known or loved the person and from knowing that the person rests with God. One can feel joy even when his or her financial situation is horrible, because he or she has the "blessed assurance" that God is "in it" somehow and that he or she is not alone. One can feel joy even when his or her feelings have been badly hurt when one enters the process of forgiveness because he or she is able to feel the healing that only God can give when one submits to God's power. Thus, what seemed so bad isn't as bad as it seemed. "Count it all joy."

Questions for Reflection and Discussion

1. Read the first chapter of James. Highlight the verses that would seem to indicate to you that forgiveness has the power to bring you spiritual peace.

2. Is having spiritual peace important to you? Or are you more likely to hold onto a grudge at the expense of that peace?

3. James 1:19–21 talks about us having to be "quick to listen, slow to speak and slow to become angry." Do these verses speak to you as to why you might be having a hard time forgiving?

4. Can you convert a situation that you have been counting as a bad thing into one of joy? What lessons have you learned from this situation?

5. List the things you're afraid of if you enter into the process of forgiveness.

6. Share a situation you had where you felt joy "in spite of" your situation.

7. Do you believe God will work with you as you struggle to forgive or do you not trust God enough with your pain to even try?

Getting Even vs. Being Healed

The driving force behind us not being able or being willing to forgive is our desire to "get even." Sometimes, in bad moments, I have had conversations with God asking permission to just be able to "get" whoever it was who "got" me. Anything less seems unfulfilling and somehow, not right. God's promise to take care of us is nice and all, but sometimes, it is not comforting. It's not comforting, not because God isn't capable of taking care of us, but because we're not capable (or willing) to let God work things out in God's own way.

The scriptures admonishing or directing us to forgive are troubling. Jesus must have known his words would not set right with us and that knowledge might have led him to say that he did not come to bring peace, but a sword. (Matthew 10:34) In the Sermon on the Mount, Matthew 5:38–41, Jesus says:

"You have heard that it was said, 'An eye for eye and a tooth for a tooth.' But I tell you, Do not resist an evil-doer. But if someone strikes you on the right cheek, turn the other side also; and if someone wants to sue you and take your coat, give your cloak as well; and if anyone forces you to go one mile, go also the second mile."

Surely, we think when we read this, Jesus jests. Jesus cannot possibly mean that he wants us not to resist evil perpetuated against us! It goes against everything we've ever been taught. How many of us have been told, "If someone hits you, hit him back!" In fact, in my house, if someone hit us and we came home crying, we stood the chance of being punished by our parents for not defending ourselves! So how can Jesus expect us to just let someone get away with hurting us?

Jesus was in effect abolishing the old Jewish law of limited vengeance cited by the Lex Talionis, or the law of "tit for tat." It works for us, doesn't it? Jesus didn't think so. Even though this law was (or is) cited at least three times in the Old Testament, (Exodus 21:23–25; Leviticus 24:19, 20 and Deuteronomy 19:21), and Jesus was well-familiar with it, he realized that following it wrought more pain than peace.

Surely scholars, priests, and scribes argued with Jesus. The law was meant for good, they would say. It was the beginning of mercy and its original aim was the limitation of vengeance. Before the law, if someone did something to someone else, an entire village or family could seek retaliation. This law limited the vengeance to the one who had been wronged. Surely Jesus knew that! Actually, the law went further; it laid out the way in which a judge might make his ruling. So, the law was never intended to give an individual the right to exact justice in his or her own way.

Furthermore, Jesus' critics might have said to him, the Lex Talionis was only part of Jewish law; there were other laws that clearly warned against people seeking vengeance against another. (Leviticus 19:18; Proverbs 24:29; Lamentations 3:30)

Still, Jesus insisted that vengeance, or revenge-seeking, hampered the process of forgiveness. The reason has to be that if one is intent on "getting even" with someone, he or she cannot be intent on getting close to Jesus the Christ. The two motives are antithetical; they cancel each other out as completely as fear cancels out faith. It must be what Jesus means when he says "No one can serve two masters; for a slave will either hate the one and love the other...." (Matthew 6:24) It is a human weakness. Jesus knew it.

Our human psyches are limited in their ability to function in a bi-polar manner. We are more unilateral than we are multi or bi-lateral. I learned this in my pastorate as I tried to function as both pastor and choir director. Anyone who knows music and the work of directing choirs knows that the choir director is expected to have a different personality than the pastor. The choir director can be brusque and demanding and impatient; the pastor is not expected or really allowed those attributes. For years, I directed the choir and had an enormous problem with my pastorate, for while the music was wonderful, the people couldn't make the separation between the two roles. On Sunday morning while I was preaching, half the time the choir would be angry at "me" the "choir director" because they would remembered my impatience during rehearsal.

They also couldn't accept the interchangeableness of the roles. As choir director, they knew me in a different way. They became "familiar" with me, which, for a leader, is not a good thing. Some people could make the distinction, but it was truly very few.

It is the same way with us in our trying to seek revenge and still be in accordance with Jesus' will. The choir members thought they were respecting me as pastor, but they couldn't. In our revenge-seeking mode, we think we're following Jesus, but we cannot. It's like the human incapacity to be happy and frown at the same time. Try it! It doesn't work. Our psyches and apparently our bodies are wired like that. So, try as we might, we cannot make two spiritually opposite forces work at the same time. To seek revenge is human; to enter into the process of forgiveness is uniquely spiritual.

Okay. We might buy the above arguments. But, we might say to Jesus, why is it that the command to forgive is not one time, but continually? In Matthew 18:21–22, scriptures read:

"Then Peter came and said to him, 'Lord, if another member of the church sins against me, how should I forgive? As many as seven times?' Jesus said to him, 'Not seven times, but, I tell you, seventy-seven times.' "

In the King James Version the command is "seventy times seven."

Why would Jesus ask us to practice unlimited forgiveness? Again, it must be because Jesus is seeking to lead us to a place of spirituality that allows us peace in spite of the wrongs done against us. A spirit of vengeance is fed by the emotions of anger and pain. No one carrying those two emotions can be peaceful. And no one can get to God carrying emotions which so completely block our spiritual veins and arteries. In Isaiah, it is written that "Those of steadfast mind you keep in peace – in peace because they trust in you." (Isaiah. 26:3). In the King James version, it reads, "thou will keep him in perfect peace, whose mind is stayed on you, because he trusteth in you." It is a fact, that when our minds are cluttered with the desire for revenge, so are our spirits and we don't get the opportunity to experience "the peace of God, which passes all understanding." (Philippians 4:7)

The question becomes, then, do we want peace or not? Sadly, when it comes to choosing whether we want to "get even" or enter into the process of forgiveness, most of us would choose the former. We would choose to die with gnarled, eaten-up spirits resulting from our taking matters into our own hands than to die with a spirit of peace, indicating a real closeness to Jesus.

Understand this: Jesus does not want any of God's children to hurt. Jesus would like for us to trust God enough to let God do the disciplining. God would like us to trust God enough to know that God sees everything that is done to us and will handle it. God wants us to stand up for what is right, but to let God handle the matters of the spirit which only God is qualified to do.

When the World Trade Center Towers were destroyed on September 11, 2001, many Americans called for revenge. Thank goodness, the leaders of the country didn't follow their urges to seek just that. The hold-up was not because this Christian nation was trying to follow Jesus' commands; it was more because we could not pinpoint exactly who to "get even" with immediately. Thus, began the war on terrorism. The desire to get even, however, still exists. It is a blow to our national ego to think that we can let Osama bin Laden or whomever it was who was responsible for that horrible day to get away with it. I shudder to think what this country and indeed the world would be like today had the revenge started on September 12, 2001.

Revenge is antithetical to peace because one vile act only produces the desire for a matching vile act on the part of the original offender. Instead of leading to a peaceful spirit, the actions of revenge lead to more spiritual distress. In cases of the death penalty, I have heard many people say that seeing the offender die gave them only momentary, temporary solace. Over time, they still felt the anger and the hurt. Jesus commanded us to forgive because the only balm for a wounded spirit is the spirit of God.

I have advised people whom I've counseled to read and pray the words of Psalm 35:1: "Contend, O Lord, with those who contend with me; fight against those who fight against me!" I advise it because I have prayed it and have actually felt God's presence within me; lifting my pain and assuring me that God had it in God's hands. It may sound stupid, but, after all, Christianity is something we must do. It must be practiced. In bad times, I have prayed the words of this Psalm for as long as I've needed, and have been given peace. My attention has been successfully diverted from those who hurt me to the God who can heal me.

All of us must make the choice as to whether or not we want to "get even" or "get healed." It is a matter of humanity versus spirituality; eternal damnation versus eternal life. Jesus won't force us to make the choice. No. The decision is all ours.

Questions for Reflection and Discussion

1. Find as many scriptures in the Old Testament as you can that admonish us to forgive others. Are you surprised at how many there are?

2. Identity the Old Testament scripture which most convicts you of the need to forgive someone. Why does it "get" to you?

3. Discuss why you think Christians don't really understand the message of forgiveness. Were you taught to forgive growing up? What were the limitations to having to forgive, as your parents taught you?

4. What have been the repercussions of your not forgiving someone? Who was it? Your mother? Father? Child? Spouse? Have you sought revenge against anyone close to you?

5. How should Christians reconcile the apparently contradictory message of forgiveness with the value of one needing always to defend oneself? Are the two values impossible to meld? Is there a way to defend oneself and still enter into the process of forgiveness?

6. What do you think would be a just way of dealing with the terrorists who attacked America? How should others who have been adversely affected by American practices seek revenge on us, or do you believe they should?

7. Study the story of Joseph and his brothers in Genesis. Do you admire Joseph or think less of him because he forgave his brothers and gave up a good opportunity to seek revenge? How would you have handled the situation?

No Repentance, No Forgiveness

I will never forget a member of my congregation one day coming to me after a sermon where I had taken great pains to explain repentance and how Jesus said we all had to repent – which merely means to change – in order to be saved.

This woman was incensed and told me that she had spoken to God and God had told her she was all right as she was. She didn't need to change. That was said to me years ago, but it still rings loudly in my ears and in my spirit and it makes me wonder how many Christians feel just the same way.

If we are Christian, the supposition may be made that we believe in Jesus and in what he said. And one thing he said was that we were all to repent or suffer the consequences. In Luke 13, we find Jesus giving this command as clearly as he can:

"At that very time there were some present who told him about the Galileans whose blood Pilate had mingled with their sacrifices. He asked them 'Do you think that because these Galileans suffered in this way they were worse sinners than all other Galileans? No, I tell you; but unless you repent, you will all perish as they did. Or those eighteen who were killed when the tower of Siloam fell on them – do you think that they were worse offenders than all the others living in Jerusalem? No, I tell you; but unless you repent, you will all perish just as they did. (Luke 13:1–5)

Clearly, Jesus wants us to know that repentance is necessary to "…enter the[realm] of heaven." (Matthew 7:21)

There is some change, some inner, spiritual preparation we must all do in order to take advantage of the [realm] of heaven, which is much more about being spiritually mature than dying and going to some tangible place. Jesus says that the realm of God is within us:

"Once Jesus was asked by the Pharisees when the [realm] of God was coming, and he answered, 'The [realm] of God is not coming with things that can be observed; nor will they say, 'Look, here it is!' or 'There it is!' For, in fact, the [realm] of God is among you." (Luke 17:20–21)

This repentance, then, is about watering and nurturing what is within us, making it grow and mature. Being repentant does not mean one has to stand on a mountain and proclaim how terribly bad he or she has been. Rather, it is recognizing that within all of us, there are weeds – impediments — that have kept God's spirit at bay, and our willingness to give in to the need for those parts of us to change represents movement toward God, toward the realm.

The problem is, we have to want it. Repentance is work, simply because we are changing something that has been in existence for a long time and with which we've grown comfortable. Our personalities, by the time we really develop a God-consciousness, are like windows which are jammed shut because of poor painting. Remember back when you entered a room and realized it was too hot or musty. All you wanted to do was open the window and get some air. Or remember when you wanted to paint a room and realized the window had to be opened to be painted. Remember pulling at the window, with no luck? You pulled and tugged, and finally realized that it was the old paint which was holding up progress. In order for the window to be opened, the old paint had to be chipped away, and it did not come away easily! Without going through the process, however, of chipping that paint away, the window would not open.

That analogy, regardless of its simplicity, is a good illustration of how our spirits are by the time we really begin to develop a deep desire for God's presence in our lives. God cannot enter in, nor can our old stuff get out, unless and until we allow the "old paint' to be chipped away. That is, nothing happens toward our spiritual growth until we enter the process of repentance!

The most important ingredient in this process is desire, our personal desire to change. (Which means, of course, we have to believe that there's a need for us to change). When one is an athlete or a dancer or a musician, one has to practice or work out. Some days, it just isn't a priority. Some days, you just don't want to practice or work out. But sooner or later, the desire to succeed, to be good at what one does, has to take precedence over the dread of the work out, and successful athletes find themselves working even harder, to make up for the lost day, and musicians find themselves practicing harder.

We as Christians have to have the desire to want to change, to repent, and to enter into the process, or we will simply languish our time away until it is too late. Consider the story of the foolish virgins, the ten who waited until it was too late to get oil for their lamps. Too late, they went to buy oil for their lamps, but:

> "...while they went to buy it, the bridegroom came, and those who were ready went in with him into the wedding banquet; and the door was shut. Later, the other bridesmaids came also, saying, 'Lord, Lord open to us.' But he replied, 'Truly I tell you, I do not know you. Keep awake therefore, for you know neither the day nor the hour." (Matthew. 25:10–13)

The virgins waited too long to change their ways, to make preparation for God's realm and lost out. Surely, some say, Jesus would not be that resolute. Who knows? All that we have is the word of God and what it says. Who among us would want to risk losing out on the blessing of God because we chose not to do what he said in ample time?

Christianity is a blueprint, a map, for achieving levels of spirituality which prepare us for God's presence. Being repentant helps us in that process, by convicting us of the need to change in order to attain the level of spirituality needed for the peace that passes all understanding. It removes from us the vestiges of human behavior which are an impediment to doing God's will.

So, in this discussion of forgiveness, of what do we have to repent in order to be willing to forgive someone? One thing would be pride. Many of us do not want to forgive because our pride won't let us. We feel that to forgive someone, especially if the offense has been terrible and a lot of people know about it, would be admitting to being a wimp. Pride has been identified as one of the seven deadly sins. In Proverbs, the writer says on God's behalf, "Pride and arrogance and the way of evil and perverted speech I hate." (Proverbs 8:13), Later in that same book, the writer observes, "Pride goes before destruction".(Proverbs 16:18) Still yet, in that same book, the writer declares, "A person's pride will bring humiliation, but one who is lowly in spirit will obtain honor." (Proverbs 29:23)

Jesus gives observations on how pride gets in the way of a relationship with God as well. He says in Matthew, "Therefore, whoever humbles himself like this child is the greatest in the Kingdom of Heaven." When he talked about the tax collector and the Pharisee in Luke, he tells the story of how the Pharisee lifted himself up as being confident in his own righteousness, and thanked God he wasn't like the riff-raff of society. The tax collector, on the other hand, recognized his faults, and asked for mercy from God. And what did Jesus say? "I tell you, this man went down to his home justified rather than the other; for all who exalt themselves will be humbled, but all who humbles themselves will be exalted." (Luke 18:14)

All through the Gospels, Jesus admonishes us to take a more lowly position, not in order to be seen as "holy" by the outside world, but in order to make one's spirit more pliable for the requirements of God and for being a part of God's realm. In James, the writer says, "Humble yourselves before the Lord, and he will exalt you." (James 4:10)

You might recoil at these scriptures. Nobody wants to take the low road. We seem to have two extremes; either we won't follow these commands of Jesus because they are too distasteful, or we "over follow" the commands and become too lowly. Some of us take on a spirit of martyrdom and allow people to walk over us. That is not what is required.

All Jesus is asking us to do is to let our pride take the back seat to the commands of God. He is not asking us to be wimps or to let people walk over us. Losing our pride helps us to make room for God's spirit in us, no matter how grievous the offense was against us.

A second thing of which we have to repent in order to even be willing to enter into the process of forgiveness is anger. Letting go of the anger means we trust God to calm us and to deal with the offender. Letting go of the anger also means we let go of the need to see our offender hurt, in our time and in our way. Anger is a powerful driving force. It destroys us, and when left untended it turns into hurt which then deepens into rage. Think of all the crimes of passion committed. Many of them came from the anger that was never given to God, with the trust that God would handle it. One of the most frustrating things about our relationship with God is that we cannot direct God's path; God has to direct ours, and the truth of the matter is that most of the time, we do not agree with his travel plan.

Anger is hard to get rid of. It takes a lot of prayer to even want to repent of it. The biggest reason is that most of us, when we're angry, feel justified, and because of that, we see no need to let go of it. As I write this, I have anger against some people whom I have loved for a while, and I have not yet prayed earnestly enough for God to take the anger in God's hands and to deal with the situations in God's way. As long as I hold onto the anger, I am not repentant, and run the risk of keeping the realm of God away from myself.

A third thing of which we need to repent in order to enter into the process of forgiveness is fear. We are often afraid of what forgiveness will look like and how we'll appear to our friends and family. There was a program on television recently where an African American fugitive was befriended by a white housewife whom he had taken as a hostage. Right in the midst of being wronged, this woman was able to forgive this man and minister to him. She ended up leading him out to be captured, seconds away from when a SWAT commander was going to give the order for the house to be ambushed. On one hand, she was afraid of what her husband and others would say about her, but on the other hand, she was living in God's realm, acting spiritually in a very dangerous human situation. The epilogue of the movie said that the fugitive served his time in prison and is still friends with the housewife. It was quite a powerful message as to what God is able to do.

If we can let go of pride, anger and fear, meaning if we can repent of those things, change those things in us, we are a step closer to being able to forgive. The way is paved for us wanting to forgive those who have wronged us. In repenting of those things, we also repent of our distrust of and in God. As I write this, I am still not able to let go of my anger against a couple of people, but I am willing to do it. I know I must do it. I've done it before and have been blessed, and I want the blessing again.

I have learned that without repentance, there can be no forgiveness.

Questions for Reflection and Discussion

1. What has been your understanding of what repentance is up to this point?

2. Do you agree or disagree with the author's definition of forgiveness? Find scriptures to support your opinions.

3. Other than pride, anger, and fear, what are some other things of which you may need to repent in order to enter into the process of forgiveness?

4. The author acknowledges a non-forgiving spirit because of anger. Are there people in your life against whom you hold anger? Why have you not been able to let the anger go?

5. Study the story of the ten wise and the ten foolish virgins in Matthew 25. Do you agree with the interpretation of the story as offered by the author?

6. Do you find it difficult to acknowledge that you are a sinner? What is your definition of sin? Do you think that because many people have such a negative conception of sin that the desire to repent on the part of many is so low?

7. What do you think of when you think of God's realm? What do you think Jesus meant when he said the realm of God is near you?

Why Forgive?

So, what's the big deal? Why do we have to forgive?

Well, aside from it being commanded by Jesus, we forgive because God has forgiven us. Let's face it. God has forgiven all of us of a lot of things. We count on, bank on, God's forgiveness of us. Jesus allows us to ask for forgiveness in the Lord's Prayer, "Forgive us our trespasses," but he also puts on the divine requirement, "…as we forgive those who trespass against us." We ask for forgiveness and we find comfort in the fact that we receive it, but we are reluctant to pass the blessing on.

Jesus says that we are to forgive "so that your Father in heaven may also forgive you your trespasses." (Mark 11:25) He says in Matthew that if we forgive people who sin against us, "your heavenly Father will also forgive you." (Matthew 6:14) In Ephesians, Paul writes, "In him we have redemption through his blood, the forgiveness of our trespasses, according to the riches of his grace that he lavished on us." (Ephesians 1:7) Later in Ephesians, Paul writes, "…And be kind to one another, tenderhearted, forgiving one other, as God in Christ has forgiven you." (Ephesians. 4:32) And in Colossians, Paul says, "Bear with one another and, if anyone has a complaint against another, forgive each other; just as the Lord has forgiven you, so you also must forgive." (Colossians 3:13) We must forgive because Jesus told us to and because he has forgiven us of a lot of things.

I have found comfort in that reality. In fact, God's forgiveness of me was probably my reason for wanting to know Jesus better. I asked for forgiveness and could actually feel the power of his forgiveness all over me. It was one of the most awesome spiritual experiences I had ever had. I was beating myself up, hating myself, calling myself names...you get the picture? But at the same time, I was talking to God. I had heard someone preach a sermon on how God accepted us just as we are — faults and all — and how he had this incredible capacity to forgive. My spirit must have been ready to receive that Word, because I absorbed the sermon. As the Word was preached, I found myself sobbing. I had reached a state of repentance. I wanted to change. I knew I would never do what I had done before again. And if I was so lucky as to be forgiven by God, I felt I'd be able to go on. I promised God that I'd give my life to God as a token of my thanks.

I had to pray for a while, weeks, maybe, before I actually felt God's presence come over me, but I knew I had been forgiven. Remarkably, in his forgiveness, he took away my capacity to absorb the non-forgiving spirits of those around me. It was as though I had been isolated, yet connected to a wonderful new fellowship. All that mattered from that point on was that I was faithful to God and God's commands. It was the most wonderful healing I had received.

When we think of how many times God has forgiven us, it can be quite moving. If God were human, with the human incapacity and unwillingness to forgive but to instead seek revenge, the world would be a lot smaller, if not demolished altogether.

Ironically, slave masters taught the lesson of forgiveness to slaves for self-serving purposes, but their teaching (which they didn't' practice themselves!) has served to keep the United States from a race war. From slave narratives to present day recollections, African Americans will tell how their parents and grandparents taught them to forgive the evil perpetuated against them. Their parents and grandparents got the lesson from the slave owners who inherently knew their actions were unacceptable to God and knew that if forgiveness were not taught, the slaves would rise in rebellion.

That lesson of forgiveness, though, while self-serving, gave the slaves exactly what they needed in order not to be consumed by anger. It brought them into the "realm of God," giving them peace in spite of brutality against them, giving them strength to hold on and to move on. It gave them room in their spirits to receive God's goodness in spite of the earth's cruelty. It allowed them to let go of their need for revenge and to press forward and learn to read and write and live in a country which sought to kill their spirits.

The slaves ability to forgive shows a big reason why we are asked to forgive: It frees our spirits up to connect with God and to move on. We don't forgive for the sake of the offender. We forgive for the sake of our own survival. We can choose to be eaten by anger and pride and fear and rage and thus diminish the quality of our human and spiritual walks, or we can forgive and experience the miracle of God's parting the Red Sea of resistance and pain within us to make room for our movement through our pain and captivity to freedom.

Who in the Bible forgave and moved on? Joseph was one. His is one of the most powerful stories of forgiveness in the Bible. His brothers had left him to die and he had been sold into slavery. He had reason to hate them forever. They had treated him badly merely because they were jealous. It was a wrong thing to do.

Time passed and the tables turned. Joseph, in spite of being treated so poorly by his own family, had been deeply blessed, and now, those who had so badly wounded him had to come to him for mercy and deliverance. He recognized his brothers; they did not know him. He listened to their needs, holding up as best he could, and then, "He turned away from them and wept; then he returned and spoke to them. And he picked Simeon and had him bound before their eyes. Joseph then gave orders to fill their bags with grain, to return every man's money to his sack, and to give them provisions for their journey. This was done for them." (Genesis 42:24, 25)

Joseph had the opportunity to get them back. Who amongst us would not have jumped at the chance? But it seems that Joseph had opened his heart to God and God's forgiveness of him had convicted him of the need to forgive his brothers. God had shown him that even though his brothers had been wrong, some of what Joseph had represented to them was not so holy either. It is a powerful story.

Others in the Bible who apparently forgave and who were thus able to move forward include Moses (Numbers 12:13), David (1 Samuel 24:17; 26:11), Elisha (2 Kings 6:22; Psalm 35:13), Stephen (Acts 7:60) and of course, Jesus (Luke 22:51; 23:34)

When we think of how much God has forgiven us, we are humbled. It's amazing that God could forgive David, for example, of adultery, for betraying one of his best friends and soldiers to cover up David's affair with his wife, and for eventually ordering his murder, and still use him! David realized that, and it moved him to forgive others in his life. His prayer, "Create in me a clean heart, O God, and put a new and right spirit within me" (Psalm 51:10) carried him. I'm sure, however, that there were many difficult moments when he didn't want to forgive. It's the knowledge of how deep God's forgiveness of us is that should inspire us to do the same, or at least try the same. And it is our desire to please God which should give us the strength to carry out the desire. God forgave Moses of murder and of being emotionally unfaithful to his wife in an attempt to save his own life. God forgave Peter for denying God and Thomas for doubting. God even forgave Judas for betrayal...not for their sakes, but for God's own. By example, Jesus showed us that forgiving others is yes, obedience to God's command, but also the way by which we can move forward and feel God's presence, no matter how bad the pain is in our lives.

If we think about how God has forgiven us, it becomes easier to forgive the father who was drunk or never around; the mother who was a prostitute and who put her need for men ahead of her needs for her child. It becomes easier to even entertain the thought of forgiving the best friend who betrayed you or the spouse who cheated on you. It even becomes easier to forgive the drunk driver who took away your only child while on a drunken binge. You can even entertain the thought because you have grown spiritually enough to know that the forgiveness will be pleasing to God and will free your spirit to get closer to God. You can forgive the husband who left you for a younger woman, or the woman who apparently only wanted you for your money. You can forgive people who blighted your spirit, kept you unemployed or underemployed. You can forgive racism, sexism, homophobia, ageism, a government who used you but neglected you and your needs when the war was over. You can forgive pastors who deceived you, priests who molested you, organizations that covered up wrong-doing. You can...and if you do, you're able to move on simply because you have moved closer to God.

Forgiving doesn't mean you lie down and die and let people walk over you. You can still move to make sure there is justice in an unjust world, but with a forgiving spirit, your actions are healthy and not toxic. People will listen to you because you speak now with the spirit of God in you and behind you. It's a different persona you present to the world, because it is less you and more the God that you let into your painful sores.

It's not easy, but it is necessary. It's definitely a faith walk. In 1 Peter 5:7, the writer says, "Cast all your anxiety on him, because he cares for you." In essence, in order to forgive, we cast all the pain, all the concerns, all the fear and anger and pride, onto the shoulders of the One who can carry it, and the reward is freedom for us. When we become free enough to forgive, we finally become free enough to live.

Questions for Reflection and Discussion

1. Talk about how you felt when you absolutely knew God had forgiven you of something you thought was terrible.

2. Study the story of Jonah and the whale. Like Jonah, do you ever get angry because God has forgiven some people that you think should not be forgiven?

3. Do you believe that God really forgives everyone?

4. If you were asked to write a letter of forgiveness to someone who hurt you badly, could you do it? Would you do it?

5. Would you be willing to jeopardize your "place" in heaven by not forgiving someone? Or do you think your place would be jeopardized at all?

6. What would it take, at this point, for you to enter into the process of forgiveness?

7. What's more important to you right now? Being right or doing God's will?

Other books from the Insights series include:

User's Guide to the Bible
Facing Change
The Bible and Spiritual Disciplines
The Bible and Decision Making
Women in the Bible
Job
Powers and Principalities
Living in Times of Crisis

Booklets in the Insights series cost $5.00 each. Orders for multiple copies will receive the following discounts: 10–24, 10% discount; 25–49, 20% discount; 50–99, 30% discount.

To order call, 1-800-537-3394;
E-mail: pilgrimpress@ucc.org;
Web site: www.pilgrimpress.com.